THE NATIONS OF THE WORLD
By Mike Donovan

Note: this first edition covers slightly less than half the countries in the world. It is focused mostly on the smaller ones.

HOLY SEE

The population of Vatican City, which is governed by the Holy See, is 801. I guess when the Pope is out of town, it shrinks to 800. This enclave within Rome is what is left of the Holy Roman Empire.

NAURU

They speak Nauruan and English on this island of 10, in the middle of nowhere. 10,824 people live here. Nauru is part of Micronesia and the nearest neighbor is 195 kilometers away.

TUVALU

11,792 people live on the Nation-Island of Tuvalu. It is ten square miles in size and the capital is Funafuti.

PALAU

18,094 people call Palau home.

Palau is a democratic republic. The Capital city is Ngerulmud.

The President of Palau is Surangel Whipps, Jr.

Palau Capitol Building

SAN MARINO

San Marino is landlocked on all sides by Italy. 33,931 people live there, a full house at Fenway Park.

It is rare in that it has two leaders, not one. Allessandra Cardelli and Merko Dolcini are Captain's Regents.

San Marino is 24 square miles big.

LIECHTENSTEIN

Sandwiched inside Austria and Switzerland is the tiny Principality of Liechtenstein, population 38,128.

Although there is a prime minister, the Prince is the power in Liechtensteing. Hans Adams II is the current prince.

Vaduz is the capital. Liechtenstein is 64 square miles small.

MONACO

Monaco is the seventh smallest country in population at 39,242. If 1100 people moved to Leichtenstein, Monaco could move up to number six. It is 0.81 square miles small.

The bottom half of the flag is white.

ST KITTS AND NEVIS

This country in the Leeward Island group became independent in 1983. 53,000 people live there. Alexander Hamilton, the man on the ten dollar bill, was born there.

The capital is Bassatere. The current prime minister is Tim Harris. St. Kitts and Nevis is 94% African.

MARSHALL ISLANDS

The Marshall Islands are 70 square miles of Pacific territory. The current president is David Kabua.

The population of the Marshalls is 59,190.

DOMINICA

The east Caribbean island of Dominica is home to 71,986 people.

The capital of Dominica is Roseau. It is 290 square miles. The current president is Charles Savarin.

ANDORRA

Lodged in the Pyrenees Mountains is the tiny nation of Andorra. The population is 77,265. The capital is Andorra la Vella.

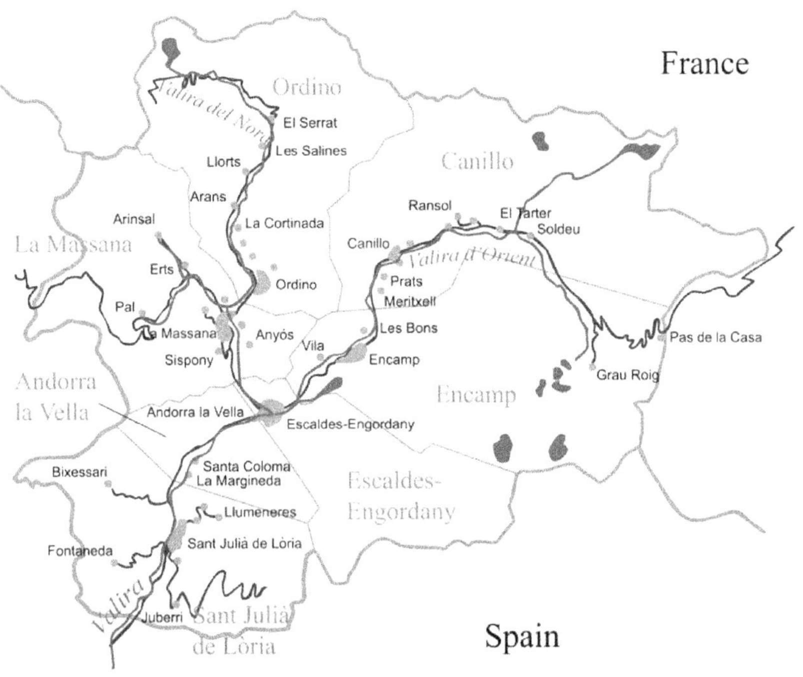

France
Spain
Ordino
Canillo
La Massana
Andorra la Vella
Escaldes-Engordany
Encamp
Sant Julià de Lòria
Valira del Nord
Valira d'Orient
Valira
El Serrat
Les Salines
Llorts
Arans
Arinsal
La Cortinada
Ransol
El Tarter
Soldeu
Canillo
Prats
Meritxell
Les Bons
Pas de la Casa
Erts
Ordino
Pal
Grau Roig
La Massana
Anyós
Vila
Encamp
Sispony
Andorra la Vella
Escaldes-Engordany
Bixessari
Santa Coloma
La Margineda
Llumeneres
Fontaneda
Sant Julià de Lòria
Juberri

ANTIGUA AND BARBUDA
Population 97,929.

Barbuda up top, Antigua on the bottom.

Flag of Antigua and Barbuda

The capital of Antigua and Barbuda is St. John's.

SEYCHELLES
Population 98,929.

The Seychelles Islands, off the east coast of Africa, has been independent since June 1976. The capital is Victoria. The sitting president as of February 26, 2021 is Wavel Ramkalawen.

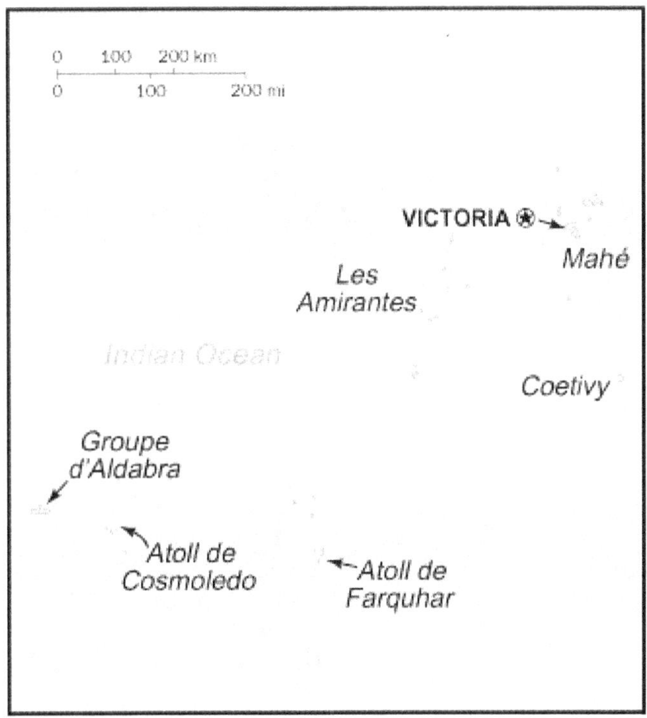

The Seychelles

TONGA

Tonga is an island nation in the South Pacific. It has been independent since 1970 and the capital is Nuku' Alofa.

The head of state is Tupou VI. Tonga is 289 square miles and 105,695 people live there.

ST VINCENT & GRENADINES

Often it is just listed among nations as St. Vincent.

The capital of St. Vincent and the Grenadines is Kingstown. The Governor General is Susan Dougan. The population of these Caribbean islands is 110,695.

GRENADA

The population of Grenada is 112,523.

Grenada, the 'Island of Spice,' is the Caribbean island that Ronald Reagan invaded in 1983. It has a population of 112,523 people. The capital is St. George's.

The Prime Minister is Keith Mitchell. It has been independent since February of 1974.

KIRIBATI
Capital: South Tarawa

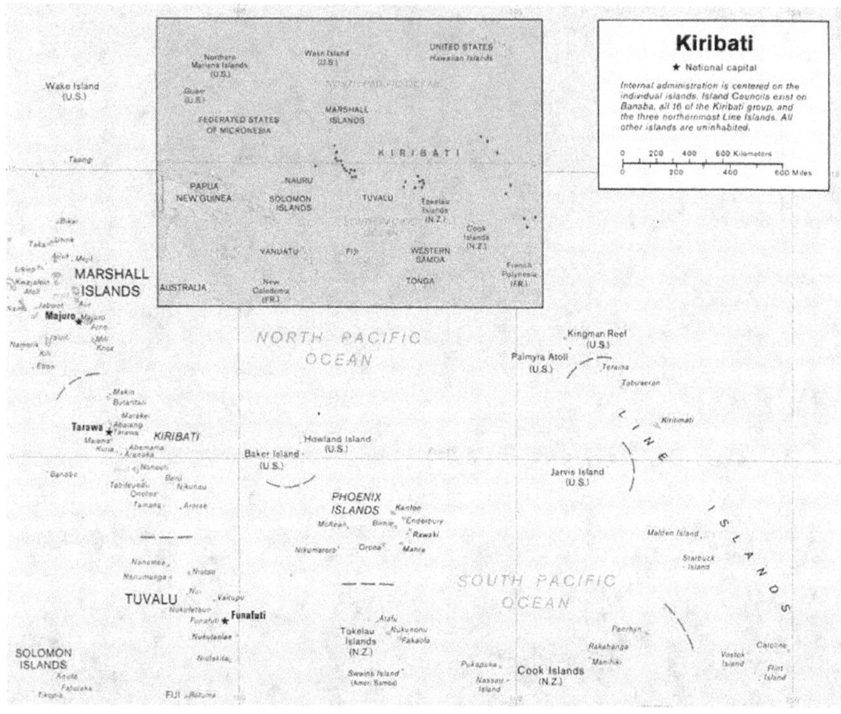

Kiribati, in the Pacific, is home to 119,000 people. It was the scene of many famous battles of WWII.

ST LUCIA

The capital of St. Lucia is Castries. The population is 183,627.

SAMOA

The population of Samoa is 198,414. The capital is Apia.

SAO TOME AND PRINCIPE

The population of Sao Tome and Principe is 259,159. The capital is Sao Tome.

BARBADOS

Population 287,607
Capital city: Bridgeton

VANAUTU

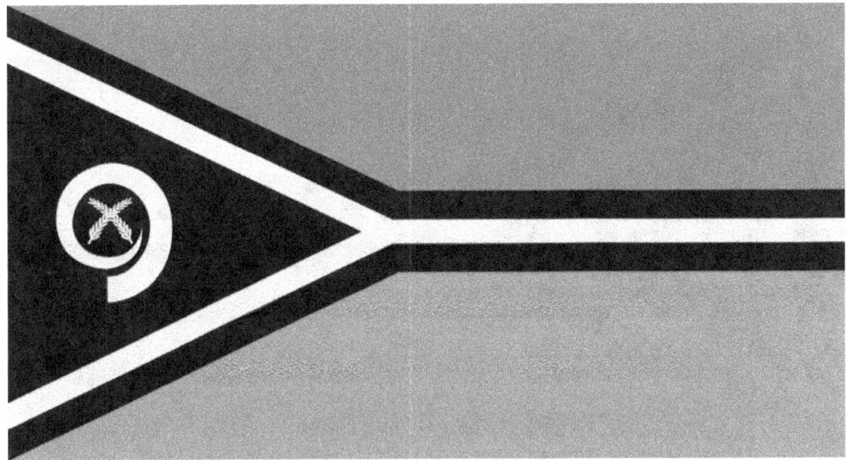

The population of Vanautu is 312,051 people.

ICELAND

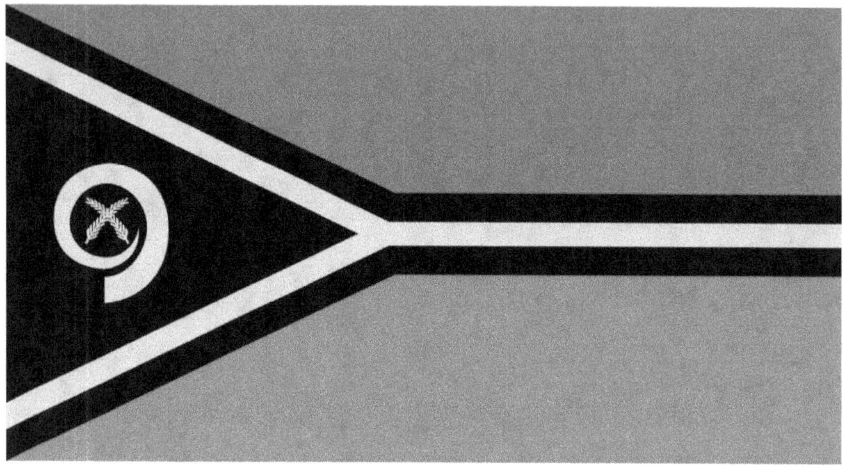

The population of Iceland is 341,243

BAHAMAS

393,244 people live in the Bahamas.

BELIZE

Belize, in Central America is 8,867 square miles and has a population of 397,628 people, mostly Mestizo.

The capital of Belize is Belmopan. The current Prime Minister is Johnny Briceno.

BRUNEI

Brunei is located on Borneo, the largest island in Asia. There are 437,000 people there.

The capital city of Brunei is Bandar Sawi Begawam.

It reached independence in 1984.

The current Sultan is Hassani Bolkiah.

MALTA

The population of Malta is 441,543. The capital is Valetta.

Malta is located in the Mediterranean Sea. It was the scene of a famous siege in World War II.

MALDIVES

The Maldives are 120 square miles of land, off the southwest coast of India. 540,544 people call it home.

The capital of Maldives is Male.

MICRONESIA

The capital of Micronesia is Palikir. The president is Dave Panuelo. The population is 548,914.

The Federates States of Micronesia fill 1,003,000 square miles of water and a mere 271 square miles of land.

Micro Flag of Micronesia

CAPE VERDE

This nation sits in the Atlantic Ocean, some 300 miles west of the tip of West Africa.

The Capital is Praia.

The current President of Cape Verde is Jorge Carlos Fonseca. There are 1,557 square miles of land.

SURINAME
The capital of Suriname is Paramaribo.

Suriname is the smallest country in South American. It is the one in the middle of that three-pack of small countries on the north coast of the continent.

The current leader is Chan Santokhi.

NORTH ATLANTIC OCEAN
Paramaribo
GUYANA
French
Guiana
(FRANCE)
SIPALIWINI
BRAZIL
Suriname
International boundary
District (district)
boundary
National capital
District (district) capital
Railroad
Road

LUXEMBOURG

The Capital of Luxembourg is Luxembourg City. 625,978 people live the life of Lux.

Colors of Luxembourg

The Prime Minister of Luxembourg is Xavier Bettel. It is bordered by France, Germany and Belgium. It is 998 square miles "large."

MONTENERGO
Population 628,066 – Capital: Podgoricia

Montenegro was attached to Serbia in 1992 and has been fully independent since 2006. It it 5,33 square miles large. The president is Milo Ducanovic.

NASA View of Montenegro

SOLOMON ISLANDS

World War II made Guadalcanal famous, and Solomon Islands Campaign decided the Pacific War.

The capital of the Solomon Islands is Honiara. There are 11,000 square miles of land in the island nation. It has been independent since 1978 and the Prime Minister is Manasseh Sogavare.

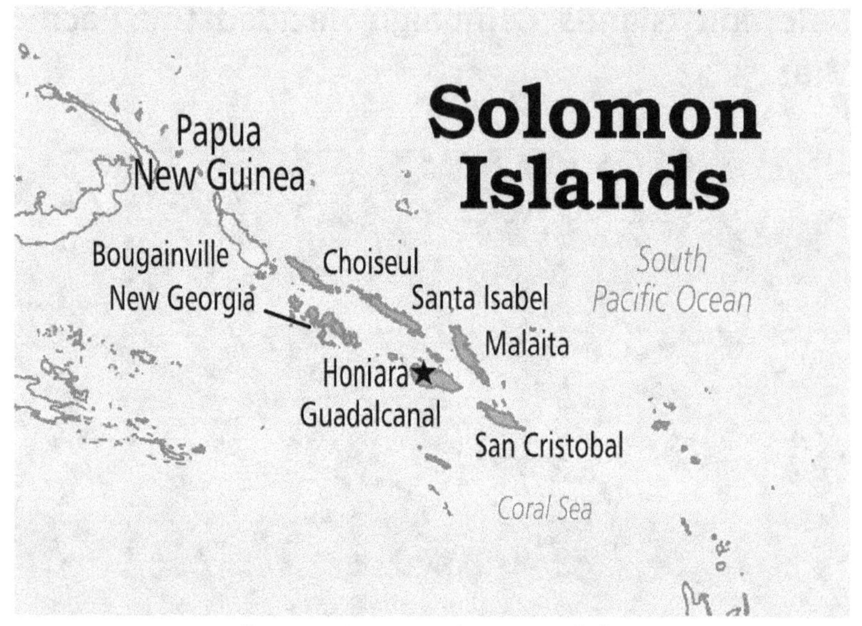

Map from Operationworld.org

BHUTAN
Population: 771,608
Capital:

Flag of Bhutan – Draw it

Below is a map of the Thunder Dragon Kingdom

GUYANA

No Jonestown jokes please! They always have a bad punch line.

The capital of this nation on the north coast of South America is Georgetown.

The population of Guyana is 786,552. The president is Irfaan Ali. This was once known as British Guyana.

COMOROS

The population of the Comoros is 869,601

The Comoros Islands are located off the east coast of Africa, and north of the great island of Mozambique.

And what is the capital of Comros? Wrong, moron, it's Moroni.

I have played at the Comoros Comedy Castle 11 weeks and the people were great.

FIJI

896,000 live in the pacific island state of Fiji. I want to go there so bad, I get fidgety just daydreaming about it.

It is in Melanesia, 1,300 miles northeast of New Zealand.

I must live there!

Fiji Flag

Fiji has been independent (of the UK) since 1970. The capital is Suva.

The President of Fiji is Jioji Konrote (below).

DJIBOUTI

Shake your Djibouti. This country is about to break the million-person barrier. There are 988,00 people there. It is bordered by Eritria, Somalia and Ethiopia.

Djibouti has been independent since June 27, 1977. It is 9,000 square miles, and the President is Ismail, Oscar Guelleh.

ERITREA
Red Sea
YEM.
Bab el Mandeb
Moussa Ali
Khor Angar
ETHIOPIA
Balho
Obock
Tadjoura
Gulf of Aden
Golfe de Tadjoura
DJIBOUTI
Lac Assal
Yoboki
Abhe Bad
Dikhil
Ali 'Sabieh
SOMALIA
0   20   40 km
0   20   40 mi

ESWATINI

1,160,164 people live in the landlocked Kingdom of Eswatini. It is surrounded by South Africa and Mozambique.

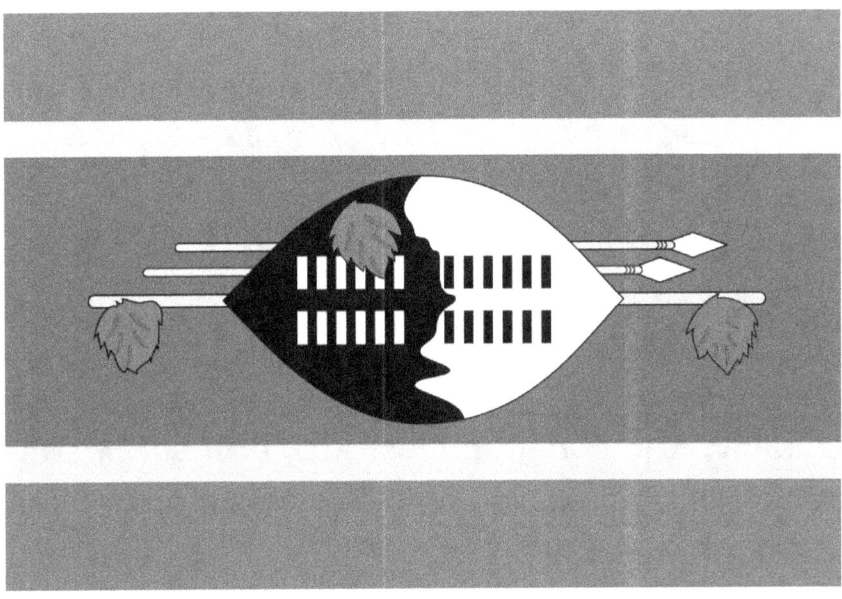

Eswatini was formerly known as Swaziland, but people confused it so often with Switzerland, that it decided, in 2018, to change it's name.

There are two capitals. The legislative capital is Lobama. The executive capital is Mbabane. It is 6,704 square miles large.

The acting Prime Minister of Eswatini is the man pictured below, Themba N. Masuku.

Sadly, the Kingdom lost it's Prime Minster, Ambrose Dlamini, to Covid 19 on December 13 of 2020. He was 52.

CYPRUS

This island nation on the eastern Mediterranean is home to 1,207,359 people.

The Flag is a Map

The capital is Nicosia. Cyprus is 3,572 square miles, and has been independent since 1960.
The current president is Nicos Anastasindes.

Cyprus was occupied by Germany during WW2

MAURITIUS
Population: 1,271,768

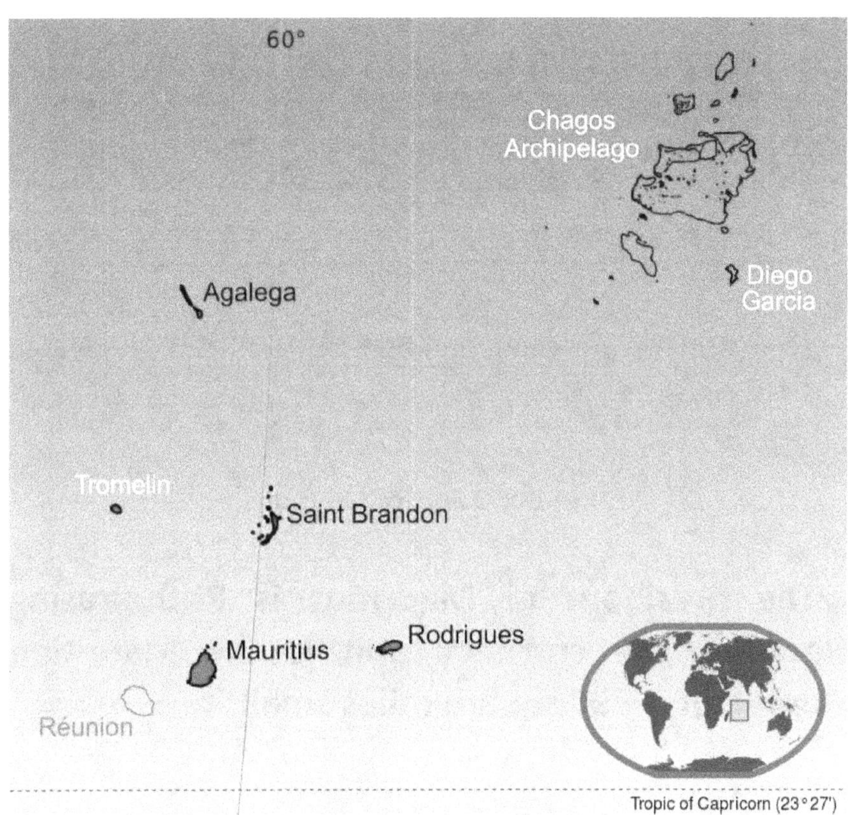

Map by Yashveer Poonit

The Four Colors of Mauritius

The president of Mauritius is Prithuirasing Roopun. The currency unit is the Mauritian Rupree. It is 790 square miles small.

TIMOR-LESTE

Timor or, East Timor, is a country of 5,974 square miles and a population of 1,318,445. Since the word 'timor' is derived from the Malay word for east, the nation is, in essence, 'East East.'

Timor became independent in 1975, but Indonesia took it away in 1976. It became independent again in 2002.

The capital is Dili and the president is a dude named Francisco Gutteres.

124
126
Banda Sea
INDONESIA
Pulau Atauro
DILI
Baucau
Liquica
Manatuto
Savu Sea
Ermera
Viqueque
Pante
Makasar
Foho
Tatamailau
Pulau
Jaco
Suai
INDONESIA
Timor Sea
0   50   100 km
0   50   100 mi

East Timor

ESTONIA

There are 1,326,535 people in Estonia. The capital is Tallinn.

The Soviets occupied Estonia in 1940 and it has been independent since August 20, 1991.

The president of Estonia is Kersti Kaljulaid. It is 17,462 square miles.

FINLAND
Gulf of Finland
Baltic Sea
Paldiski
Muuga
Kunda
Narva
TALLINN
Kohtla-Järve
Hiiumaa
Haapsalu
Paide
Lake Peipus
Saaremaa
Pärnu
Tartu
Viljandi
RUSSIA
Võrts-Järv
Irbe Strait
Gulf of Riga
Valga
Suur Munamägi
Lake Pskov
LATVIA
0   60 km
0   50 mi

Estonia

TRINIDAD AND TOBAGO
Population: 1,339,488
Capital: Port-of-Spain

Trinidad and Tobago is 1,981 square miles of Carribbean island land. The president of Trinidad and Tobago is Paula-Mae Weekes.

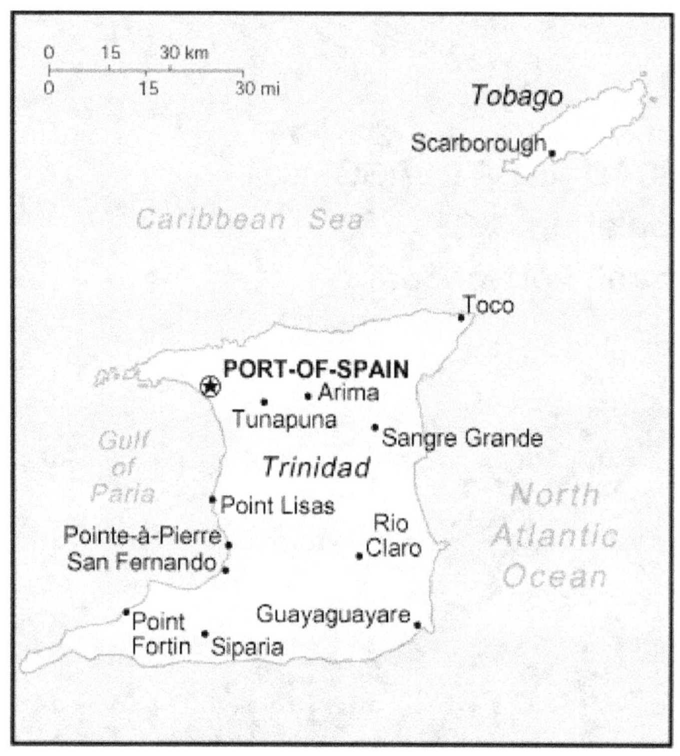

0   15   30 km
0   15   30 mi
Tobago
Scarborough
Caribbean Sea
Toco
PORT-OF-SPAIN
Arima
Tunapuna
Sangre Grande
Gulf
of
Paria
Trinidad
Point Lisas
Rio
Claro
Pointe-à-Pierre
San Fernando
North
Atlantic
Ocean
Point
Fortin
Siparia
Guayaguayare

EQUATORIAL GUINEA

There are 1,402,985 people in Equatorial Guinea at

The capital of Equatorial Guinea is Malabo, but a new capital is almost completed and some of the government has already moved there. The new capital will be Cuidad de la Paz.

Equatorial Guinea is 10,830 square miles. The president is Teodoro Manque.

MALABO
Luba
Isla de Bioko
CAMEROON
Bight
of
Biafra
Ebebiyin
Bata
Mongomo
Island not shown in true
geographical position
Isla de Annobón
Mbini
Evinayong
Acalayong
Isla de Corisco
Corisco Bay
GABON

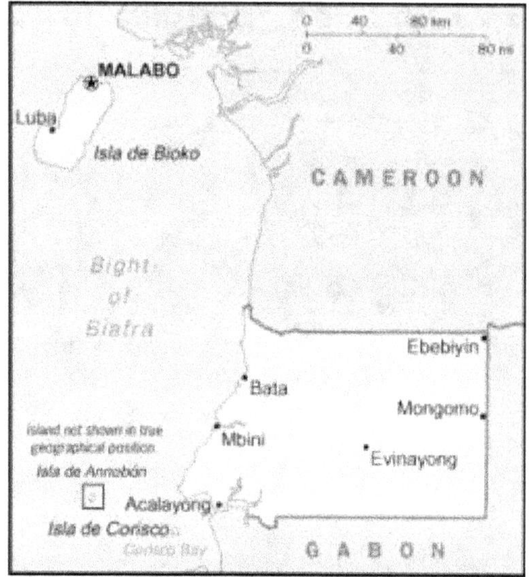

E.G.

BAHRAIN

The island nation of Bahrain has been independent since 1971. The capital is Manama.

The Prime Minister or Bahrain is Salman bin Hamad al Khalifa. It is 300 square miles small.

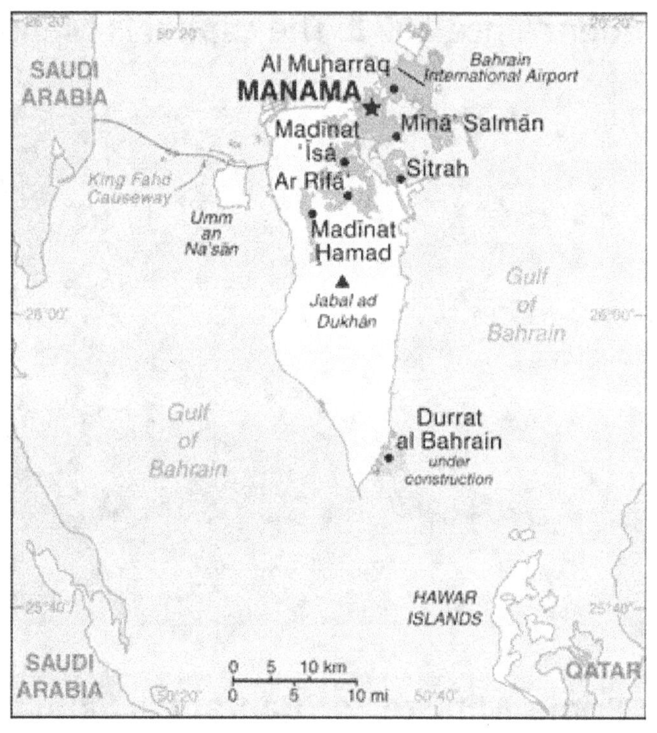

SAUDI ARABIA
Al Muḥarraq
MANAMA
Bahrain International Airport
Madīnat ʿĪsā
Mīnāʾ Salmān
Ar Rifāʿ
Sitrah
King Fahd Causeway
Umm an Naʿsān
Madīnat Hamad
Jabal ad Dukhān
Gulf of Bahrain
Gulf of Bahrain
Durrat al Bahrain
under construction
HAWAR ISLANDS
SAUDI ARABIA
QATAR
0   5   10 km
0   5   10 mi

LATVIA

Capital: Riga
Population: 1,866,198
Square Miles: 24,198

The current president of Latvia is Egils Levits. Latvia became independent (of the USSR) during the 'August Coup' of 1991.

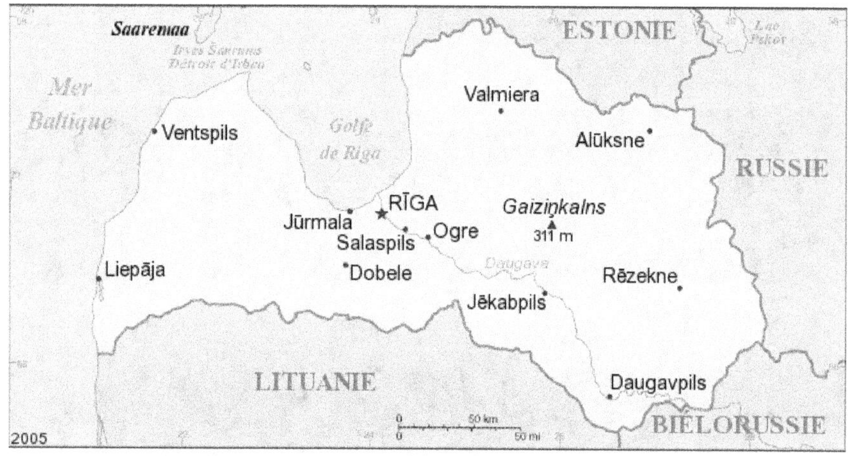

Latvia was occupied by the USSR in 1940

GUINEA BISSAU

Guinea Bissau, bordered by Sengal and Guinea, is 13,948 square miles, and home to 1,968,001 people.

Guinea Bissau has been independent since 1974. The current president is Umaro S. Embalo.

Guinea Bissau

SLOVENIA

2,078,938 people live in Slovenia, a nation of 7,827 square miles.

The President of Slovenia is Borut Pahor. It became independent of Yugoslavia in 1991 and joined the UN in 1992.

The capital is Ljubljana.

Austria
Hungary
Italy
Slovenia
Ljubljana
Croatia
Gulf of
Venice
Adriatic Sea

NORTH MACEDONIA

The population of NM is 2,083,374. Skopje is the capital.

North Macedonia has been independent (from Yugoslavia) since September 8, 1991.

The President of North Macedonia is Stevo Pendarovski.

North Macedonia: 9,928 Sq. Mi.

LESOTHO

Lesotho is completely surrounded by South Africa, the largest (11,720 sq. mi.) country in the world that exists within another country (San Marino and the Holy See are the other two.)

The capital of Lesotho is Maseru. The Prime Minister (as of 2021) is Moeketsi Majoro.

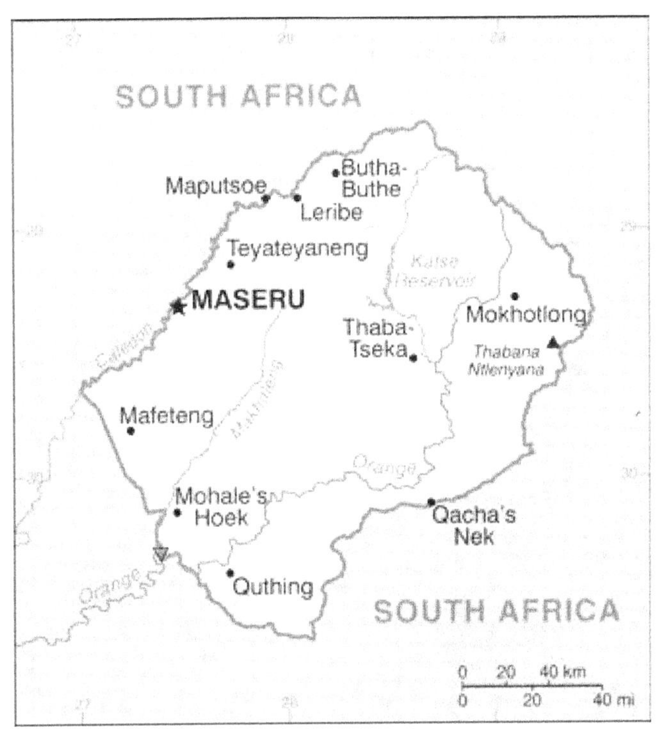

SOUTH AFRICA
Maputsoe
Butha-
Buthe
Leribe
Teyateyaneng
Katse
Reservoir
MASERU
Mokhotlong
Thaba-
Tseka
Thabana
Ntlenyana
Mafeteng
Mohale's
Hoek
Qacha's
Nek
Quthing
SOUTH AFRICA
0   20   40 km
0   20   40 mi

GABON
Population: 2,225,734

Gabon is on the west coast of lower Africa. The capital is Libreville. Gabon is 103,347 square miles and the current leader is President Ali Bongo Ondimba.

Independent since 1960, Gabon has had only three presidents!

KAMERUN
Zatoka Biafra
GWINEA RÓWNIKOWA
REPUBLIKA KONGO
Oyem
Makokou
LIBREVILLE
Owendo
Kango
Booué
Port-Gentil
Lambaréné
Lastoursville
Franceville
Mouila
Tchibanga
REPUBLIKA KONGO
Mayumba
Ocean Atlantycki
0   50   100 km
0   50   100 mi

BOTSWANA

There are 2,351,627 people in Botswana. The capital, and largest city, is Gabarone. Botswana shares a border with South Africa, Namibia and Zimbabwe.

The president of Botswana is Mokgweetsi Masisi. It is a large country of 224,610 square miles.

ANG.
ZAM.
Lake
Kariba
Caprivi Ziple
(Caprivi Strip)
Kasane
Popavalle
(Popa Falls)
Tsodilo
Hills
ZIMBABWE
OKAVANGO DELTA
Maun
NAM.
Ghanzi
Francistown
Selebi-Phikwe
Serowe
Mamuno
Mahalapye
KALAHARI
DESERT
Molepolole
GABORONE
Kanye
Tshabong
SOUTH AFRICA
0 50 100 km
0   50   100 mi

GAMBIA
Population: 2,416,668
Capital: Banjul

'The Gambia' is the formal name of Gambia. Senegal swallows Gambia. It is almost completely surrounded by Senega. The President of the Gambia is Adama Barrow. It became independent of Britain in 1965.

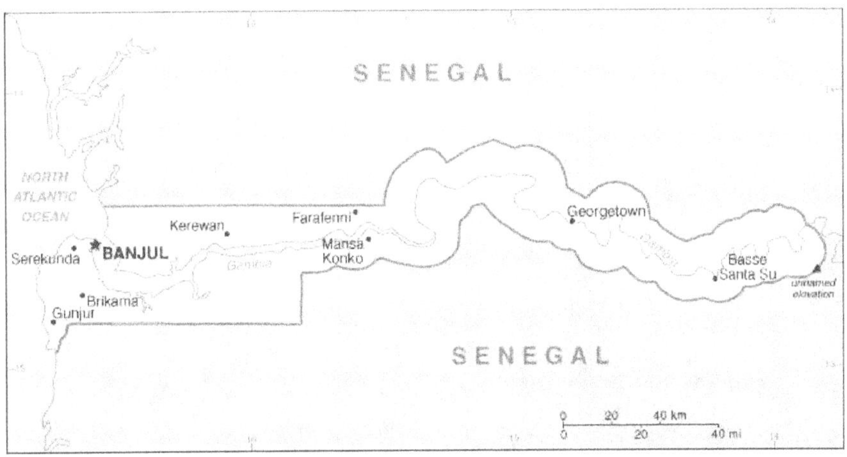
SENEGAL
NORTH
ATLANTIC
OCEAN
Kerewan
Farafenni
Georgetown
Serekunda
BANJUL
Mansa
Konko
Basse
Santa Su
unnamed
elevation
Brikama
Gunjur
Gambia
SENEGAL
0   20   40 km
0   20   40 mi

NAMIBIA

There are 2,540,905 Namibians. The capital city is Windhoek. I have a Facebook friend in Namibia named Sylvia.

The beautiful flag of Namibia

Namibia became independent of South Africa in 1990. The current head of state is President Hage Geingob. The land of Namibia is 318,772 square miles.

ANGOLA
ZAMBIA
Katima
Mulilo
Caprivi Zipel
(Caprivi Strip)
Oshakati
Rundu
Tsumeb
Popavalle
(Popa Falls)
Khorixas
Otjiwarongo
Königstein
NAMIB
WINDHOEK
Swakopmund
Gobabis
BOTSWANA
Walvis Bay
Rehoboth
KALAHARI
DESERT
SOUTH
ATLANTIC
OCEAN
DESERT
Mariental
Keetmanshoop
Lüderitz
SOUTH
AFRICA
Orange
Oranjemund
0   100 200 km
0   100   200 mi

LITHUANIA
Population: 2,722,289
Capital: Vilnius

Lithuania is 25,200 square miles. The current president is Gitanas Nauseda.

Baltic
Sea
LATVIA
Mažeikiai
Šiauliai
Būtingė
Klaipėda
Panevėžys
Utena
Kėdainiai
Jonava
Nemunas
Kaunas
VILNIUS
RUSSIA
(Kaliningrad Oblast)
Marijampolė
Alytus
Aukštojas
POLAND
BELARUS
Nyoman
0   30   60 km
0   30   60 mi

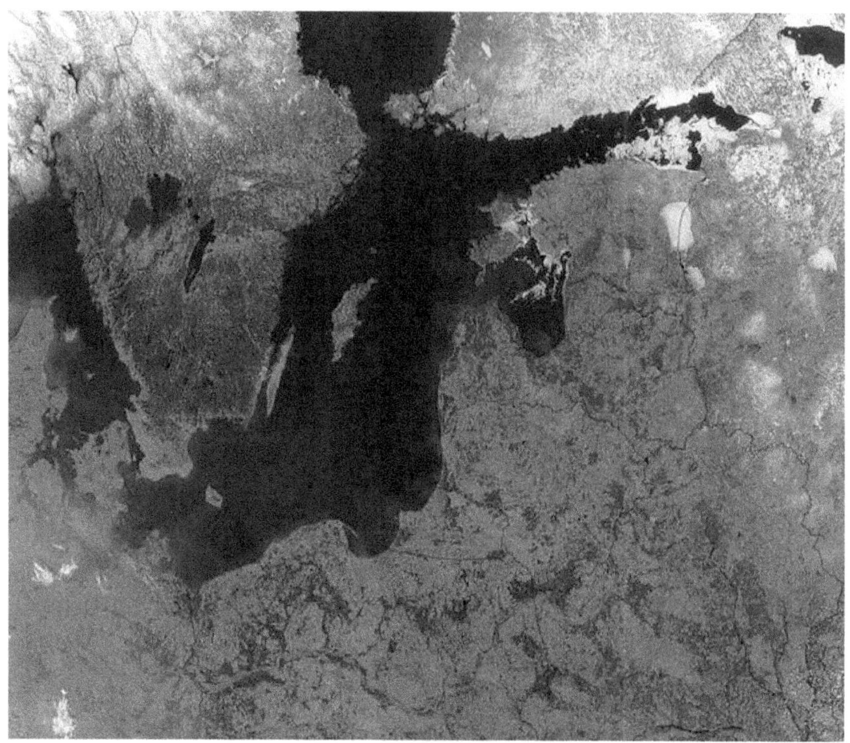

Satellite Lithuania

ALBANIA

The capital of Albania is Tirana. Italy occupied Albania in 1939, months before the German attack on Poland.

The President of Albania is Ilir Meter. It is 11,100 square miles. The population is 2,877,797.

CRO.
MONTENEGRO
KOSOVO
SER.
19
20
21
42
42
Shkodër
Maja e Korabit
Shëngjin
NORTH
MACEDONIA
Adriatic
Sea
TIRANA
Durrës
Elbasan
41
41
Fier
Korçë
Berat
Vlorë
Strait of
Otranto
ITALY
Gjirokastër
GREECE
40
40
Sarandë
0   20   40 km
Ionian Sea
0   20   40 mi
19
20
21

QATAR

Qatar has been independent since 1971. The capital is Doha.

The extra wide sized flag of Qatar

The Prime Minister of Qatar is Khalid Bin Khalifa. Qatar is 4,471 square miles of east Arabia.

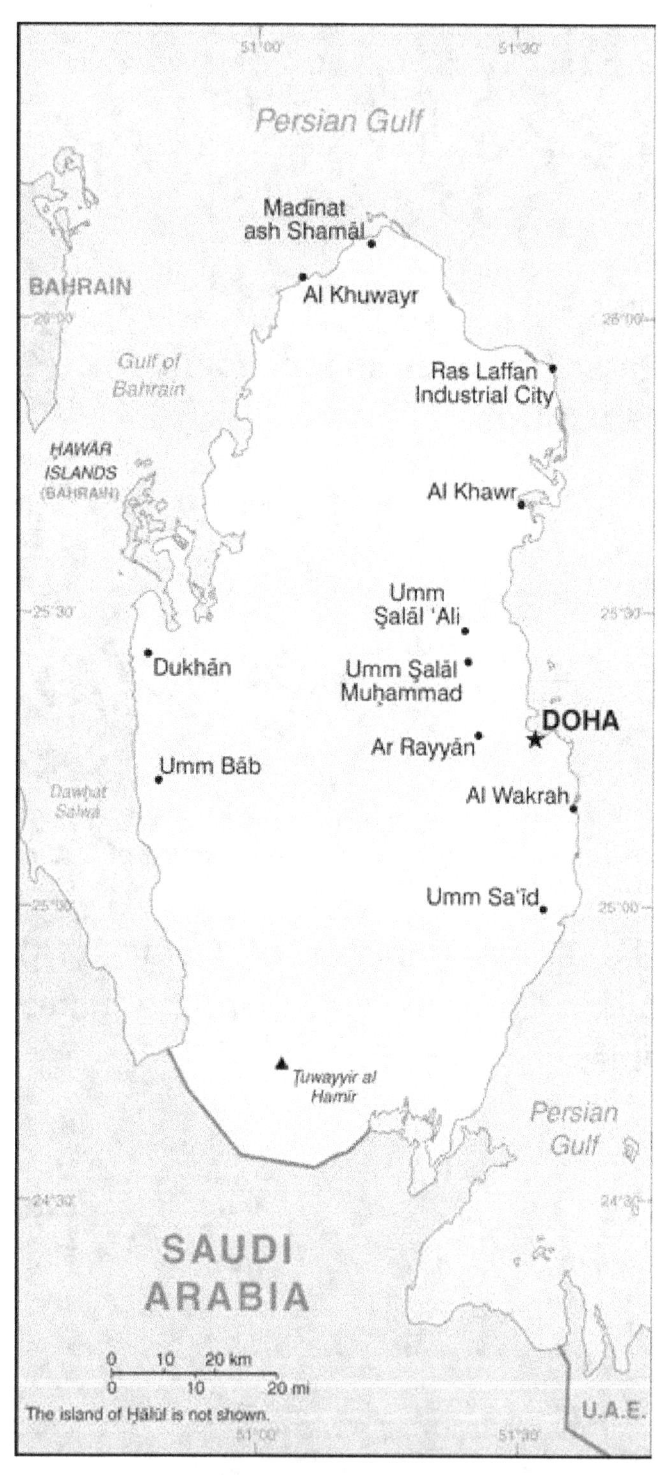

Persian Gulf
Madīnat
ash Shamāl
BAHRAIN
Al Khuwayr
Gulf of
Bahrain
Ras Laffan
Industrial City
HAWAR
ISLANDS
(BAHRAIN)
Al Khawr
Umm
Şalāl 'Ali
Dukhān
Umm Şalāl
Muḥammad
DOHA
Ar Rayyān
Umm Bāb
Al Wakrah
Dawḥat
Salwá
Umm Sa'īd
Ṭuwayyir al
Ḥamīr
Persian
Gulf
SAUDI
ARABIA
0   10   20 km
0   10   20 mi
The island of Ḥālūl is not shown.
U.A.E.

JAMAICA

I married my wife on a beach in Jamaica in 1998. Roger and Denisha were the witnesses. I wonder how they are doing?

2,961,167 people live in Jamaica. Kingston is the capital. The current prime minister is Andrew Holness.

A James Bond (Connery) movie was filmed in Jamaica. I think it was Doctor No.

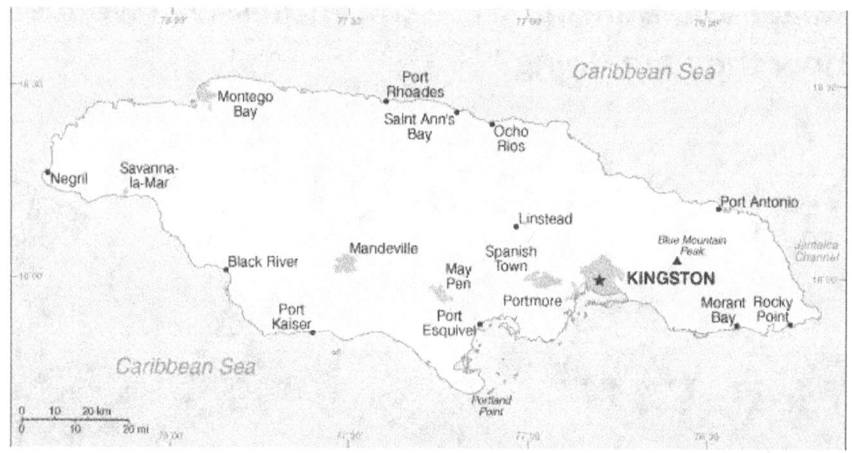

Jamaica - No Problem, Man

ARMENIA

Armenia is home to 2,963,243 people. The capital is Yerevan.

The President of Armenia is Arman Sarkissian. It is 11,484 square miles in size. Armenia became independent of the USSR on September 23, 1991.

GEORGIA
Kura
LESSER
Alaverdi
Debed
Gyumri
Vanadzor
Ijevan
Aragats
Lermagagat
Hrazdan
AZERBAIJAN
Abovyan
Lake
Sevan
Ejmiatsin
Hrazdan
Aras
Vardenis
Armavir
YEREVAN
CAUCASUS
Artashat
TURKEY
Goris
MTS
Naxçivan
(Nakhichevan)
AZER.
Kapan
Aras
IRAN
0   20   40 km
0   20   40 mi

MONGOLIA

Ulan Bator is capital of landlocked Mongolia.

The President of Mongolia is Khaltmaagiin Battulga. The country is 605,000 square miles, in between Russia and China.

Japan and Russia fought large tank battles there in 1939, prior to the September 1 beginning of the Second World War.

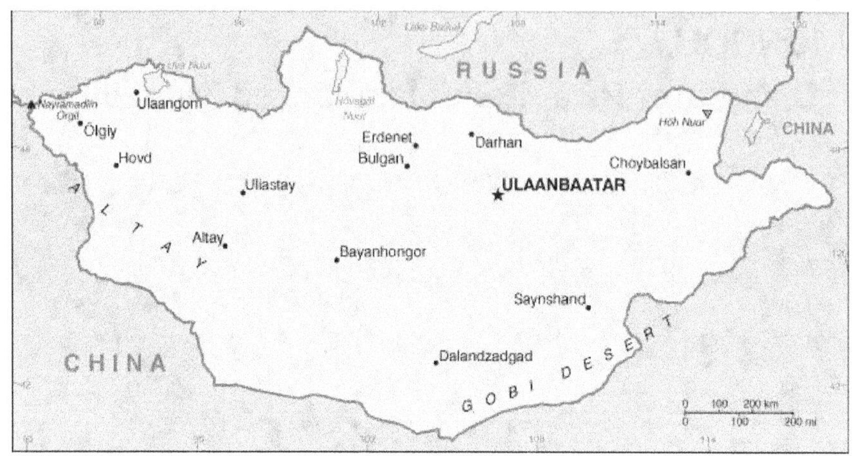
RUSSIA
CHINA
CHINA
Nayramadlin
Orgil
Ölgiy
Ulaangom
Hovd
Uliastay
Altay
Erdenet
Bulgan
Darhan
Hoh Nuur
Choybalsan
ULAANBAATAR
Bayanhongor
Saynshand
Dalandzadgad
GOBI DESERT
ALTAY
0 100 200 km
0 100 200 mi

BOSNIA AND HERZEGOVINA

Once part of Yugoslavia, Bosnia and Herzegovina won its independence in March of 1992. The capital is Sarajevo.

The High Representative is Valentin Inzko. It is 19,741 square miles.

The population is 3,280,819.

Bosnia and Herzegovina

URUGUAY

The population of Uruguay is 3,473,730. The president is Luis Lacalle Pou.

Uruguay gained its independence from Brazil in 1828. It is 64,037 square miles. The capital is Montevideo.

0   50   100 km
0   50   100 mi
Uruguay
Rio Cuareim
Artigas
Rivera
BRAZIL
Salto
Tacuarembó
ARG.
Paysandú
Embalse de Rincón del Bonete
Rio Negro
Melo
Embalse de Paso de Palmar
Fray Bentos
Treinta y Tres
Mercedes
Durazno
Laguna Merín
San José
Florida
Cerro Catedral
Colonia
Minas
Las Piedras
Rocha
Maldonado
Rio de la Plata
MONTEVIDEO
SOUTH ATLANTIC OCEAN

Uruguay

ERITREA

The President of Eritrea is Isaias Afwerki.

The population of Eritrea is 3,546,421. The capital is Asmara. Eritrea became independent of Ethiopia in 1993. It is 45,400 square miles.

SAUDI
ARABIA
SUDAN
Red
Sea
Nak'fa
DAHLAK
ARCHIPELAGO
Keren
Ak'ordat
Massawa
ASMARA
Mendefera
Badme
Soira
Tio
Kulul
YEMEN
Demarcation
Decision
Line
DANAKIL
DEPRESSION
Southern limit of the
former UN Temporary
Security Zone
Assab
Lake
Tana
ETHIOPIA
Doumera
Island
DJIBOUTI
0   50   100 km
0   50   100 mi

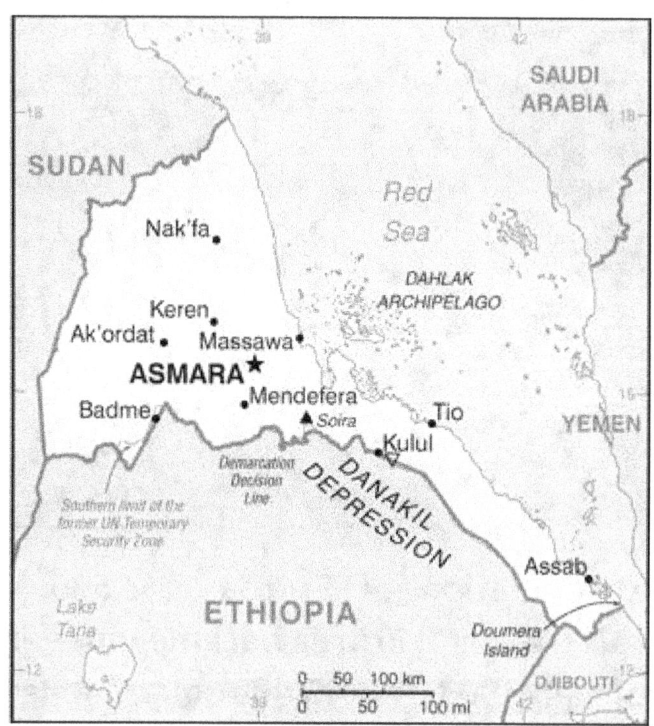

Eritrea

GEORGIA

The capital of Georgia is Tbilisi. The President of Georgia is Salome

The population of Georgia is 3,989,167. It is 26,900 square miles and became independent of the USSR the day the USSR dissolved itself: Christmas Day, 1991.

ABKHAZIA
Sokhumi
Kodori Gorge
Och'amch'ire
Zugdidi
Senaki
K'ut'aisi
P'ot'i
KOLKHET'IS DABLOBI
Sup'sa
Bat'umi
AJARIA
Akhalts'ikhe
Akhalk'alak'i
Mt'a Shkhara
GREATER CAUCASUS MOUNTAINS
RUSSIA
SOUTH OSSETIA
Ts'khinvali
Pankisi Gorge
Kura
Gori
TBILISI
Rust'avi
LESSER CAUCASUS MTS
Kura
AZER.
AZERBAIJAN
ARMENIA
TURKEY
Black Sea
0   20   40 km
0   20   40 mi

Georgia

MOLDOVA

The capital of Moldova is Chisinau.

Moldova is 13,068 square miles and has a population of 4,033,963 people. The President of Moldova is Maia Sandu. It became independent of the USSR on August 27, 1991.

0 20 40 km
0 20 40 mi
UKRAINE
Nistru Dniester
Briceni
Bălţi
Rîbniţa
TRANSNISTRIA
Nistrul (Dniester)
Prut
Dealul Bălăneşti
Dubăsari
CHIŞINĂU
Bender
Tiraspol
Cahul
UKRAINE
ROMANIA
Ozero Yalpuh
Danube
Danube
Mouths of the Danube
Black Sea

Moldova

TAIWAN

The capital of Taiwan is Taipei. The largest city is New Taipei.

Is Taiwan a country? Officially the UN does not recognize it, but 23,588,378 people live there and they think it is a country.

New Taipei Skyline

This book is dedicated to Queenie, the fastest dog alive!

And what is the greatest country in the world? That's an easy one. It's whichever country you call 'home.'

9 798715 839749